Alvin Singleton

b.1940

In Our Own House

for Soprano Saxophone, Trumpet,
Piano and Snare Drum

ED 30071

www.schott-music.com

Mainz · London · Madrid · New York · Paris · Prague · Tokyo · Toronto
© 1998 SCHOTT MUSIC CORPORATION, New York · Printed in USA

Commissioned by pianist Karen Walwyn for her Dark Fires (Vol. 2) Albany Records
CD recording with Rodney Mack, Branford Marsalis & Jason Marsalis

IN OUR OWN HOUSE

Alvin Singleton (1998)

ED30071

Soprano Saxophone

Commissioned by pianist Karen Walwyn for her Dark Fires (Vol. 2) Albany Records
CD recording with Rodney Mack, Branford Marsalis & Jason Marsalis

IN OUR OWN HOUSE

Alvin Singleton (1998)

Soprano Saxophone

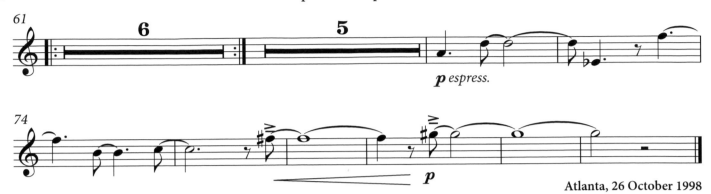

Atlanta, 26 October 1998

Trumpet in B♭

Commissioned by pianist Karen Walwyn for her Dark Fires (Vol. 2) Albany Records
CD recording with Rodney Mack, Branford Marsalis & Jason Marsalis

IN OUR OWN HOUSE

Alvin Singleton (1998)

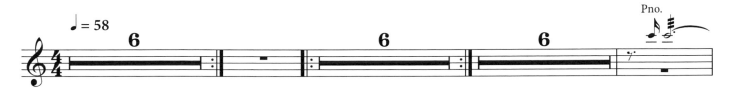

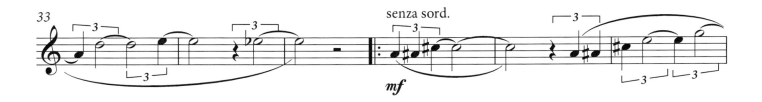

Trumpet in B♭

Atlanta, 26 October 1998

Snare Drum

*Commissioned by pianist Karen Walwyn for her Dark Fires (Vol. 2) Albany Records
CD recording with Rodney Mack, Branford Marsalis & Jason Marsalis*

IN OUR OWN HOUSE

Alvin Singleton (1998)

61 *(improvise freely, quoting previously performed material)*

65   *(stop suddenly)*   **12**

                                                              Atlanta, 26 October 1998

Piano

Commissioned by pianist Karen Walwyn for her Dark Fires (Vol. 2) Albany Records
CD recording with Rodney Mack, Branford Marsalis & Jason Marsalis

IN OUR OWN HOUSE

Alvin Singleton (1998)

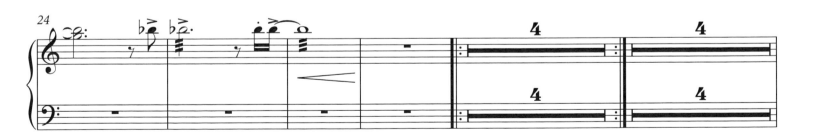

Piano

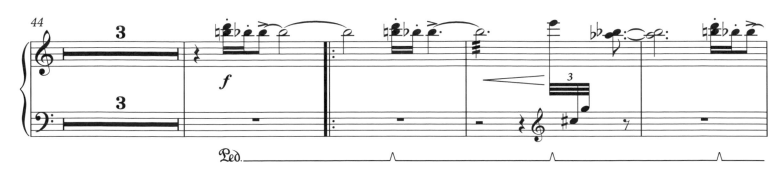

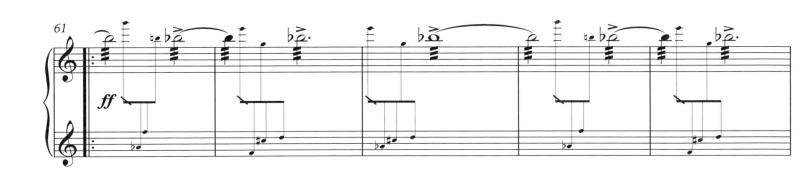

Atlanta, 26 October 1998

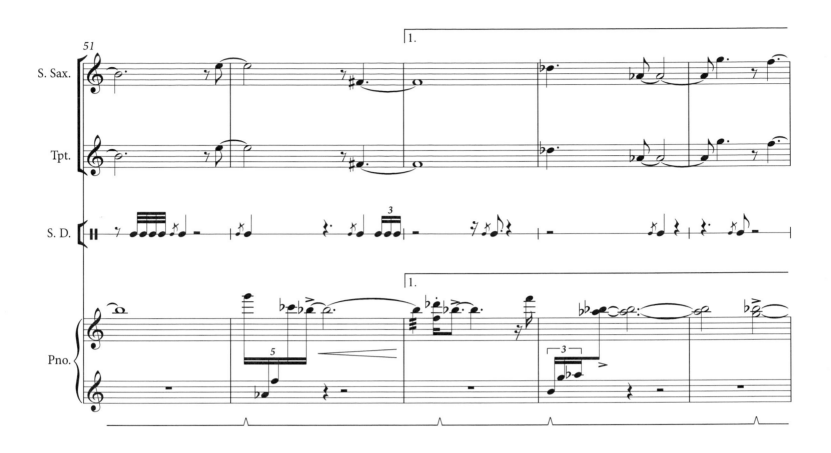

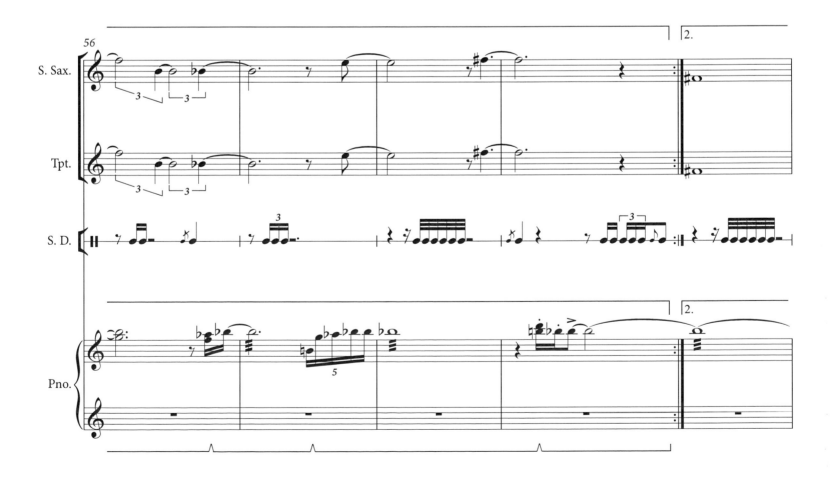

4

Atlanta, 26 October 1998